EASY APPLE COOKBOOK

50 DELICIOUS APPLE RECIPES

By
Chef Maggie Chow
Copyright © by Saxonberg Associates

Published by
BookSumo, a division of Saxonberg Associates
http://www.booksumo.com/

INTRODUCTION

Welcome to *The Effortless Chef Series*! Thank you for taking the time to download the *Easy Apple Cookbook.* Come take a journey with me into the delights of easy cooking. The point of this cookbook and all my cookbooks is to exemplify the effortless nature of cooking simply.

In this book we focus on Apple. You will find that even though the recipes are simple, the taste of the dishes is quite amazing.

So will you join me in an adventure of simple cooking? If the answer is yes (and I hope it is) please consult the table of contents to find the dishes you are most interested in. Once you are ready jump right in and start cooking.

— Chef Maggie Chow

TABLE OF CONTENTS

ANY ISSUES? CONTACT ME

If you find that something important to you is missing from this book please contact me at maggie@booksumo.com.

I will try my best to re-publish a revised copy taking your feedback into consideration and let you know when the book has been revised with you in mind.

:)

— Chef Maggie Chow

LEGAL NOTES

COMMON ABBREVIATIONS

cup(s)	C.
tablespoon	tbsp
teaspoon	tsp
ounce	oz.
pound	lb

*All units used are standard American measurements

CHAPTER 1: EASY APPLE RECIPES

SIMPLY DIVINE APPLES

Ingredients

- 1/4 C. butter
- 4 large tart apples - peeled, cored and sliced 1/4 inch thick
- 2 tsp cornstarch
- 1/2 C. cold water
- 1/2 C. brown sugar
- 1/2 tsp ground cinnamon

Directions

- In a large skillet, melt the butter on medium heat and cook the apples for about 6-7 minutes, stirring continuously.
- In a bowl, mix together the water and cornstarch.
- Add the cornstarch mixture and stir to combine.
- Stir in the brown sugar and cinnamon and boil for about 2 minutes, stirring occasionally.
- Serve warm.

Amount per serving (8 total)

Timing Information:

Preparation	5 m
Cooking	15 m
Total Time	20 m

Nutritional Information:

Calories	143 kcal
Fat	5.9 g
Carbohydrates	24.3g
Protein	0.4 g
Cholesterol	15 mg
Sodium	45 mg

* Percent Daily Values are based on a 2,000 calorie diet.

Indescribably Yummy Apple Dumplings

Ingredients

- 2 large Granny Smith apples, peeled, cored and cut each apple in 8 wedges
- 2 (10 oz.) cans refrigerated crescent roll dough
- 1 C. butter
- 1 1/2 C. white sugar
- 1 tsp ground cinnamon
- 1 (12 fluid oz.) can Mountain Dew

Directions

- Set your oven to 350 degrees F before doing anything else and grease a 13x9-inch baking dish.
- Separate the crescent roll dough into triangles.
- Place 1 apple wedge over a dough piece and roll the triangle around the apple wedge.
- With your hands, pinch to seal the roll.

- Arrange the dumplings onto the prepared baking dish in a single layer.
- In a small pan, melt the butter and add the cinnamon and sugar and stir to combine.
- Place the butter mixture over the dumplings evenly and top with the Mountain Dew.
- Cook everything in the oven for about 35-45 minutes.

Amount per serving (16 total)

Timing Information:

Preparation	20 m
Cooking	45 m
Total Time	1 h 5 m

Nutritional Information:

Calories	333 kcal
Fat	19 g
Carbohydrates	38.5g
Protein	2.7 g
Cholesterol	31 mg
Sodium	360 mg

* Percent Daily Values are based on a 2,000 calorie diet.

MOIST APPLE SNACK

Ingredients

- 1 C. sifted all-purpose flour
- 1 tsp baking powder
- 1/4 tsp salt
- 1/4 tsp ground cinnamon
- 1/4 C. butter, melted
- 1/2 C. packed brown sugar
- 1/2 C. white sugar
- 1 egg
- 1 tsp vanilla extract
- 1/2 C. chopped apple
- 1/2 C. finely chopped walnuts
- 2 tbsp white sugar
- 2 tsp ground cinnamon

Directions

- Set your oven to 350 degrees F before doing anything else and lightly, grease a 9x9-inch baking dish.
- In a large bowl, sift together the flour, baking powder, 1/4 tsp of cinnamon and salt.
- In another bowl, add the butter, 1/2 C. of white sugar and brown sugar and mix till smooth.
- Add the egg and vanilla and stir to combine.

- Add the egg mixture into the flour mixture and mix till well combined.
- Fold in the apples and walnuts and transfer the mixture onto the prepared baking dish evenly.
- In a small bowl, mix together the remaining white sugar and cinnamon and sprinkle over the apple mixture.
- Cook everything in the oven for about 25-30 minutes.
- Remove everything from the oven and keep aside to cool completely.
- Cut everything into equal sized squares and serve.

Amount per serving (16 total)

Timing Information:

Preparation	25 m
Cooking	30 m
Total Time	55 m

Nutritional Information:

Calories	143 kcal
Fat	5.7 g
Carbohydrates	22.1g
Protein	1.8 g
Cholesterol	19 mg
Sodium	94 mg

* Percent Daily Values are based on a 2,000 calorie diet.

HEALTHIER APPLE & OAT CRISP

Ingredients

- 10 C. apples, peeled, cored and sliced
- 1 C. white sugar
- 1 tbsp all-purpose flour
- 1 tsp ground cinnamon
- 1/2 C. water
- 1 C. quick-cooking oats
- 1 C. all-purpose flour
- 1 C. packed brown sugar
- 1/4 tsp baking powder
- 1/4 tsp baking soda
- 1/2 C. butter, melted

Directions

- Set your oven to 350 degrees F before doing anything else and lightly, grease a 13x9-inch baking dish.
- Place the apple slices in the bottom of the prepared baking dish evenly.
- In a bowl, mix together white sugar, cinnamon and 1 tbsp of the flour and sprinkle over the apple slices evenly.
- Drizzle the water over the apple slices evenly.
- In another bowl, add the remaining ingredients and mix till a coarse crumb forms.

- Spread the crumb mixture over the apple slices evenly and cook everything in the oven for about 45 minutes.

Amount per serving (12 total)

Timing Information:

Preparation	30 m
Cooking	45 m
Total Time	1 h 20 m

Nutritional Information:

Calories	316 kcal
Fat	8.4 g
Carbohydrates	60.5g
Protein	2.4 g
Cholesterol	20 mg
Sodium	98 mg

* Percent Daily Values are based on a 2,000 calorie diet.

ENGLISH TEATIME APPLE TREAT

Ingredients

- 2 tbsp lemon juice
- 4 C. water
- 4 Granny Smith apples - peeled, cored and sliced
- 2 tbsp butter
- 1 C. brown sugar
- 1 tsp ground cinnamon
- 1 tbsp cornstarch
- 1 tbsp water
- 1 (17.25 oz.) package frozen puff pastry sheets, thawed
- 1 C. confectioners' sugar
- 1 tbsp milk
- 1 tsp vanilla extract

Directions

- Set your oven to 400 degrees F before doing anything else.
- In a large bowl, mix together the apple slices, lemon juice and 4 C. of the water and keep aside before using.
- Drain the apple slices completely.
- In a large skillet, melt the butter on medium heat and cook the apple slices for about 2 minutes, stirring continuously.
- Stir in the cinnamon and brown sugar and cook everything for about 2 minutes, stirring continuously.

- In a bowl, mix together 1 tbsp of the water and cornstarch.
- Add the cornstarch mixture into the skillet and cook, stirring for about 1 minute.
- Remove from the heat and keep aside to cool slightly.
- Unfold the pastry sheets and cut each one into a large square.
- Cut each large square into 4 small squares.
- Divide the apple mixture in the center of each square and fold into a triangle shape, by turning from the corner to corner.
- With your hands, pinch the edges to seal tightly.
- Arrange the turnovers onto a baking sheet in a single layer about 1-inch apart and cook everything in the oven for about 25 minutes.
- Remove everything from the oven and keep aside to cool completely.
- Meanwhile for the glaze in a small bowl, mix together the remaining ingredients.
- Pour the glaze over the turnovers and serve.

Amount per serving (8 total)

Timing Information:

Preparation	30 m
Cooking	25 m
Total Time	55 m

Nutritional Information:

Calories	562 kcal
Fat	25.9 g
Carbohydrates	80g
Protein	4.8 g
Cholesterol	8 mg
Sodium	184 mg

* Percent Daily Values are based on a 2,000 calorie diet.

CHILDHOOD MEMORY DIP FOR APPLE SLICES

Ingredients

- 1 (8 oz.) package cream cheese
- 1/2 C. brown sugar
- 1 tbsp vanilla extract

Directions

- In a bowl, add all the ingredients and mix till the sugar is dissolved completely and smooth.

Amount per serving (8 total)

Timing Information:

Preparation	5 m
Cooking	5 m
Total Time	10 m

Nutritional Information:

Calories	137 kcal
Fat	9.8 g
Carbohydrates	9.8g
Protein	2.1 g
Cholesterol	31 mg
Sodium	86 mg

* Percent Daily Values are based on a 2,000 calorie diet.

AMERICAN APPLE PIE

Ingredients

- 4 C. thinly sliced apples
- 1/4 C. orange juice
- 3/4 C. all-purpose flour
- 1 C. white sugar
- 1/2 tsp ground cinnamon
- 1/4 tsp ground nutmeg
- 1 pinch salt
- 1/2 C. butter

Directions

- Set your oven to 375 degrees F before doing anything else and lightly, grease a 9-inch pie dish.
- Arrange the apple slices in the bottom of the prepared pie dish evenly and drizzle with the orange juice.
- In a bowl, mix together the remaining ingredients except the butter.

- With a pastry cutter, cut the butter in the flour mixture and mix till a coarse crumb forms.
- Place the crumb mixture over the apple slices evenly and cook everything in the oven for about 45 minutes.
- Serve warm.

Amount per serving (8 total)

Timing Information:

Preparation	30 m
Cooking	45 m
Total Time	1 h 15 m

Nutritional Information:

Calories	278 kcal
Fat	11.8 g
Carbohydrates	43.5g
Protein	1.6 g
Cholesterol	31 mg
Sodium	83 mg

* Percent Daily Values are based on a 2,000 calorie diet.

New England Apple Cookies

Ingredients

- 2 C. all-purpose flour
- 1 tsp baking soda
- 1 tsp ground cinnamon
- 1 tsp ground cloves
- 1/2 tsp ground nutmeg
- 1/2 tsp salt
- 1/2 C. softened butter
- 1 1/2 C. packed brown sugar
- 1 egg, beaten
- 1 C. chopped walnuts
- 1 C. chopped apples
- 1 C. raisins
- 2/3 C. confectioners' sugar
- 1 tbsp milk

Directions

- Set your oven to 350 degrees F before doing anything else and line the cookie sheets with parchment papers.
- In a large bowl, sift together the flour, baking soda, spices and salt.
- In another bowl, add the butter and beat till fluffy and light.
- Add the egg and sugar and mix till well combined.

- Add the egg mixture into the flour mixture and mix till well combined.
- Fold in the apples, raisins and walnuts.
- With a teaspoon, place the mixture onto the prepared cookie sheets in a single layer about 1 1/2-inches apart.
- Cook everything in the oven for about 12-14 minutes.
- Remove everything from the oven and keep aside on wire racks to cool completely.
- Meanwhile for the glaze in a small bowl, mix together the remaining ingredients.
- Pour the glaze over the cookies and serve.

Amount per serving (60 total)

Timing Information:

Preparation	30 m
Cooking	12 m
Total Time	1 h 18 m

Nutritional Information:

Calories	77 kcal
Fat	2.8 g
Carbohydrates	12.7g
Protein	0.9 g
Cholesterol	7 mg
Sodium	55 mg

* Percent Daily Values are based on a 2,000 calorie diet.

APPLE BREAD IN OGUNQUIT STYLE

Ingredients

- cooking spray
- 3 C. all-purpose flour
- 1 tsp baking soda
- 1 tsp salt
- 1 C. chopped walnuts
- 3 C. apples - peeled, cored, and chopped
- 1 C. vegetable oil
- 2 C. white sugar
- 3 eggs, beaten
- 2 tsp ground cinnamon

Directions

- Set your oven to 300 degrees F before doing anything else and grease 2 (8 1/2x4 1/2-inch) loaf pans.
- In a large bowl, mix together the flour, baking soda, cinnamon and salt.

- In another bowl, add the eggs, sugar and oil and beat till well combined.
- Add the egg mixture into the flour mixture and mix till well combined.
- Fold in the apples and walnuts.
- Transfer the mixture onto the prepared loaf pans evenly and cook everything in the oven for about 90 minutes or till a toothpick inserted in the center comes out clean.
- Remove everything from the oven and keep aside for about 10 minutes to cool before removing from the loaf pans.

Amount per serving (16 total)

Timing Information:

Preparation	20 m
Cooking	1 h 30 m
Total Time	2 h

Nutritional Information:

Calories	377 kcal
Fat	19.6 g
Carbohydrates	47.4g
Protein	4.8 g
Cholesterol	35 mg
Sodium	238 mg

* Percent Daily Values are based on a 2,000 calorie diet.

MEXICAN STYLE APPLE DESSERT

Ingredients

- 1 (21 oz.) can apple pie filling
- 6 (8 inch) flour tortillas
- 1 tsp ground cinnamon
- 1/2 C. butter
- 1/2 C. white sugar
- 1/2 C. brown sugar
- 1/2 C. water

Directions

- Set your oven to 350 degrees F before doing anything else and lightly, grease a large baking dish.
- Divide the pie filling in the center of each tortilla evenly and sprinkle with the cinnamon.
- Roll each tortilla, tucking in the edges and arrange them into the prepared baking dish, seam-side down.
- In a pan, mix together the remaining ingredients on medium heat.

- Bring everything to a boil, stirring continuously.
- Reduce the heat and simmer for about 3 minutes.
- Place the butter mixture over the enchiladas evenly and cook everything in the oven for about 20 minutes.

Amount per serving (6 total)

Timing Information:

Preparation	10 m
Cooking	30 m
Total Time	1 h

Nutritional Information:

Calories	530 kcal
Fat	18.9 g
Carbohydrates	88.2g
Protein	4.6 g
Cholesterol	41 mg
Sodium	392 mg

* Percent Daily Values are based on a 2,000 calorie diet.

COMFORTING APPLES

Ingredients

- 8 Granny Smith apples, peeled, cored, and sliced
- 2 tbsp white sugar
- 1 tsp lemon juice
- 1/4 C. cinnamon red hot candies

Directions

- In a large microwave-safe bowl, mix together all the ingredients.
- Microwave on high for about 15 minutes, stirring every 5 minutes.
- Serve warm or refrigerate to chill.

Amount per serving (8 total)

Timing Information:

Preparation	5m
Cooking	15m
Total Time	20m

Nutritional Information:

Calories	110 kcal
Fat	0.2 g
Carbohydrates	28.8g
Protein	0.4 g
Cholesterol	0 mg
Sodium	4 mg

* Percent Daily Values are based on a 2,000 calorie diet.

Danish Apple Pastries

Ingredients

Dough:

- 2 C. all-purpose flour
- 2 tbsp packed brown sugar
- 1 tsp salt
- 1 1/2 tsp instant yeast
- 3/4 C. hot water
- 2 tbsp butter at room temperature

Filling:

- 2 1/2 C. apples - peeled, cored, and chopped

- 3 tbsp butter
- 1/2 C. packed brown sugar
- 1 1/2 tbsp all-purpose flour
- 1/4 tsp salt
- 1/4 tsp ground cinnamon
- 1/4 tsp ground nutmeg

Glaze:

- 2 tbsp butter
- 2/3 C. confectioners' sugar
- 1/2 tsp vanilla extract
- 4 tsp milk

Directions

- In a large bowl, mix together 1 C. of the flour, instant yeast, 2 tbsp of the brown sugar and 1 teaspoon of the salt.
- Add the butter and water and beat till well combined.
- Add the remaining flour and beat till well combined.
- Place the dough onto lightly floured surface and with your hands, knead the dough for about 10 minutes.
- Make a large ball from the dough and place into a greased bowl.
- Turn the dough ball in the bowl evenly.
- With plastic wrap, cover the bowl and keep aside for about 1 hour.
- Meanwhile for the filling, in a bowl, mix together 1 1/2 tbsp of the flour, 1/2 C. of the brown sugar, cinnamon, nutmeg and 1/4 tsp of the salt.
- In a medium pan, mix together 3 tbsp of the butter, apples and the flour mixture on medium-high heat.
- Bring everything to a boil and reduce the heat to low.
- Simmer for about 5 minutes and remove everything from the heat, then keep aside to cool completely.
- Now, place the dough onto a floured surface and with your hands, punch it down.
- Cover and keep everything on a floured surface for about 15 minutes.
- With a rolling pin, roll the dough into a 13x8-inch rectangle.

- Arrange the dough rectangle onto a greased baking sheet.
- Carefully, turn the baking sheet onto a smooth surface.
- Place the filling mixture over the center third of the dough.
- With a sharp knife, make the cuts in the dough along the right side, starting each cut about 1/4 inch from the filling mixture.
- Cut to the edge of the dough strip, with each cut angled to about 4 o'clock.
- Each strip of dough should be about 1-inch thick.
- Repeat with the left side of the dough, angling the cuts to 8 o'clock.
- From the top, fold the dough strips across the filling mixture, alternating left and right.
- With your hands, pinch the top and bottom ends of the pastry to seal in the filling.
- With a plastic wrap, cover the pastry and keep it at room temperature for about 30-40 minutes.
- Set your oven to 375 degrees F.
- Arrange the pastry on the baking sheet and cook everything in the oven for about 10 minutes.
- Now, cover everything with a sheet of foil and cook it all in the oven for about 10 minutes more.
- Remove everything from the oven and keep it aside to cool completely.
- Meanwhile for the glaze in a pan, heat the butter on medium heat.

- Cook everything for about 5 minutes, swirling the pan occasionally.
- Transfer into a bowl and keep aside to cool slightly.
- Add the vanilla extract and confectioners' sugar and stir to combine.
- Slowly, add the milk, stirring continuously till well combined.
- Pour the glaze over the pastry and serve.

Amount per serving (8 total)

Timing Information:

Preparation	1 h
Cooking	20 m
Total Time	2 h 35 m

Nutritional Information:

Calories	337 kcal
Fat	10.6 g
Carbohydrates	57.7g
Protein	4 g
Cholesterol	27 mg
Sodium	443 mg

* Percent Daily Values are based on a 2,000 calorie diet.

Thanksgiving Apple Stuffing

Ingredients

- 1 1/2 C. cubed whole wheat bread
- 3 3/4 C. cubed white bread
- 1 lb. ground turkey sausage
- 1 C. chopped onion
- 3/4 C. chopped celery
- 2 1/2 tsp dried sage
- 1 1/2 tsp dried rosemary
- 1/2 tsp dried thyme
- 1 Golden Delicious apple, cored and chopped
- 3/4 C. dried cranberries
- 1/3 C. minced fresh parsley
- 1 cooked turkey liver, finely chopped
- 3/4 C. turkey stock
- 4 tbsp unsalted butter, melted

Directions

- Set your oven to 350 degrees F before doing anything else.
- In a large baking sheet, place the bread cubes in a single layer and cook everything in the oven for about 5-7 minutes.
- Place the toasted bread cubes in a large bowl.
- Heat a large skillet on medium heat and cook the sausage and onion till browned, breaking up the sausage into small pieces.

- Stir in the celery and herbs and cook, stirring continuously for about 2 minutes.
- Add the sausage mixture in the bowl with bread cubes.
- Add the liver, apple, cranberries and parsley and mix well.
- Drizzle with the melted butter and broth and gently stir to combine.

Amount per serving (10 total)

Timing Information:

Preparation	15 m
Cooking	25 m
Total Time	1 h 40 m

Nutritional Information:

Calories	235 kcal
Fat	11.6 g
Carbohydrates	21.7g
Protein	12.5 g
Cholesterol	80 mg
Sodium	548 mg

* Percent Daily Values are based on a 2,000 calorie diet.

Keeper Apple Butter

Ingredients

- 5 1/2 lb. apples - peeled, cored and finely chopped
- 4 C. white sugar
- 2 tsp ground cinnamon
- 1/4 tsp ground cloves
- 1/4 tsp salt

Directions

- In a slow cooker, place all the ingredients and mix well.
- Set the slow cooker on High and cook, covered for about 1 hour.
- Now, set the slow cooker on Low and cook, covered for about 9-11 hours.
- Uncover the slow cooker and cook everything for about 1 hour more.
- With a hand beater, smooth the butter and transfer into sterilized containers.
- Cover tightly and preserve in the refrigerator.

Amount per serving (128 total)

Timing Information:

Preparation	30 m
Cooking	11 h
Total Time	11 h 30 m

Nutritional Information:

Calories	34 kcal
Fat	0 g
Carbohydrates	9g
Protein	0.1 g
Cholesterol	0 mg
Sodium	5 mg

* Percent Daily Values are based on a 2,000 calorie diet.

Countryside Apple Pie

Ingredients

- 1 (9 inch) deep dish pie crust
- 5 C. apples - peeled, cored and thinly sliced
- 1/2 C. white sugar
- 3/4 tsp ground cinnamon
- 1/3 C. white sugar
- 3/4 C. all-purpose flour
- 6 tbsp butter

Directions

- Set your oven to 400 degrees F before doing anything else.
- In an unbaked pie shell, place the sliced apples.
- In a small bowl, mix together 1/2 C. of the sugar and cinnamon and sprinkle over the apple slices.
- In another bowl, mix together the flour and the remaining sugar.
- With a pastry cutter, cut the butter and mix till a crumbly mixture forms.

- Place the mixture over the apple slices evenly and cook everything in the oven for about 40 minutes.

Amount per serving (8 total)

Timing Information:

Preparation	30 m
Cooking	40 m
Total Time	1 h 10 m

Nutritional Information:

Calories	358 kcal
Fat	16.4 g
Carbohydrates	52g
Protein	2.5 g
Cholesterol	23 mg
Sodium	210 mg

* Percent Daily Values are based on a 2,000 calorie diet.

FALL SEASON APPLE MUFFINS

Ingredients

- 2 1/2 C. all-purpose flour
- 2 C. white sugar
- 1 tbsp pumpkin pie spice
- 1 tsp baking soda
- 1/2 tsp salt
- 2 eggs, lightly beaten
- 1 C. canned pumpkin puree
- 1/2 C. vegetable oil
- 2 C. peeled, cored and chopped apple
- 2 tbsp all-purpose flour
- 1/4 C. white sugar
- 1/2 tsp ground cinnamon
- 4 tsp butter

Directions

- Set your oven to 350 degrees F before doing anything else and lightly, grease 18 cups of muffin trays.
- In a large bowl, sift together 2 1/2 C. of the flour, baking soda, 2 C. of the sugar, pumpkin pie spice and salt.
- In another bowl, add the eggs, oil and pumpkin and beat till well combined.
- Add the egg mixture into the flour mixture and mix till well combined.

- Fold in the apples and transfer the mixture onto the prepared muffin cups evenly.
- In another bowl, mix together the remaining flour, sugar and cinnamon.
- With a pastry cutter, cut the butter and mix till a coarse crumb forms.
- Place the mixture over each muffin evenly and cook everything in the oven for about 35-40 minutes or till a toothpick inserted in the center comes out clean.

Amount per serving (18 total)

Timing Information:

Preparation	15 m
Cooking	45 m
Total Time	1 h

Nutritional Information:

Calories	249 kcal
Fat	8 g
Carbohydrates	42.6g
Protein	2.8 g
Cholesterol	23 mg
Sodium	182 mg

* Percent Daily Values are based on a 2,000 calorie diet.

APPEALING APPLE BEVERAGE

Ingredients

- 1 (32 fluid oz.) bottle apple juice, chilled
- 1 (12 fluid oz.) can frozen cranberry juice concentrate
- 1 C. orange juice
- 1 1/2 liters ginger ale
- 1 apple,

Directions

- In a large punch bowl, add the apple juice, orange juice and cranberry juice concentrate and stir till dissolved completely.
- Slowly, pour the ginger ale on top.
- Cut the apple thinly in vertical slices.
- Place the apple slices on the top in the punch bowl.

Amount per serving (12 total)

Timing Information:

Preparation	10 m
Cooking	10 m
Total Time	10 m

Nutritional Information:

Calories	168 kcal
Fat	0.1 g
Carbohydrates	42.1g
Protein	0.2 g
Cholesterol	0 mg
Sodium	19 mg

* Percent Daily Values are based on a 2,000 calorie diet.

Easiest Apple Crisp

Ingredients

- 4 C. apples - peeled, cored, and sliced
- 1 tsp ground cinnamon
- 1 C. white sugar
- 3/4 C. all-purpose flour
- 1/2 C. cold butter

Directions

- Set your oven to 350 degrees F before doing anything else and lightly, grease an 8x8-inch casserole dish.
- Place the apple slices in the bottom of the prepared baking dish evenly.
- Sprinkle with the cinnamon and drizzle with the water evenly.
- In a bowl, mix together the sugar and flour.
- With a pastry cutter, cut the butter and mix till a crumbly mixture forms.

- Place the mixture over the apple slices evenly and cook everything in the oven for about 30-40 minutes.

Amount per serving (6 total)

Timing Information:

Preparation	20 m
Cooking	40 m
Total Time	1 h

Nutritional Information:

Calories	361 kcal
Fat	15.6 g
Carbohydrates	55.7g
Protein	2 g
Cholesterol	41 mg
Sodium	110 mg

* Percent Daily Values are based on a 2,000 calorie diet.

ELEGANT APPLE & CHEDDAR STUFFED CHICKEN BREAST

Ingredients

- 2 skinless, boneless chicken breasts
- 1/2 C. chopped apple
- 2 tbsp shredded Cheddar cheese
- 1 tbsp Italian-style dried bread crumbs
- 1 tbsp butter
- 1/4 C. dry white wine
- 1/4 C. water
- 1 tbsp water
- 1 1/2 tsp cornstarch
- 1 tbsp chopped fresh parsley, for garnish

Directions

- In a bowl, mix together the apple, breadcrumbs and cheese.
- Place the chicken breasts between 2 sheets of wax paper and with a meat mallet, flatten to 1/4-inch thickness.

- Place the mixture in the center of the chicken breasts evenly.
- Roll each breast around the filling and secure with the toothpicks.
- In a large skillet, melt the butter on medium heat and cook the chicken breasts till browned completely.
- Add the wine and 1/4 C. of the water and simmer, covered for about 15-20 minutes.
- Transfer the chicken breasts onto a plate.
- In a bowl, mix together the cornstarch and the remaining water.
- Add the cornstarch mixture in the skillet with juices and cook till the gravy becomes thick.
- Pour the gravy over the chicken breasts and serve with a garnishing of parsley.

Amount per serving (4 total)

Timing Information:

Preparation	15 m
Cooking	25 m
Total Time	40 m

Nutritional Information:

Calories	139 kcal
Fat	5.1 g
Carbohydrates	4.9g
Protein	15 g
Cholesterol	46 mg
Sodium	120 mg

* Percent Daily Values are based on a 2,000 calorie diet.

Scrumptious Pork Chops with Apple

Ingredients

- 4 (3/4 inch) thick pork chops
- 1 tsp vegetable oil
- 2 tbsp brown sugar
- salt and pepper to taste
- 1/8 tsp ground cinnamon
- 1/8 tsp ground nutmeg
- 2 tbsp unsalted butter
- 2 tart apples - peeled, cored and sliced
- 3 tbsp pecans (optional)

Directions

- Set your oven to 175 degrees F before doing anything else and place a medium baking dish in the oven to warm.
- Lightly, brush the pork chops with the oil.
- Heat a large skillet on medium-high heat and cook the chops for 5-6 minutes, flipping occasionally.

- Now, transfer the chops into a warm baking dish and place everything in the oven.
- In a small bowl, mix together the brown sugar, nutmeg, cinnamon, salt and black pepper
- In the same skillet, melt the butter and stir in the apples and brown sugar mixture.
- Cook, covered till the apples become soft.
- With a slotted spoon, transfer the apple slices to a plate.
- Divide the apple slices over the chops evenly and again keep everything in the oven to stay warm.
- Cook the sauce till it becomes slightly thick.
- Pour the sauce over the chops and serve.

Amount per serving (4 total)

Timing Information:

Preparation	20 m
Cooking	25 m
Total Time	45 m

Nutritional Information:

Calories	262 kcal
Fat	16 g
Carbohydrates	17.1g
Protein	13.8 g
Cholesterol	48 mg
Sodium	27 mg

* Percent Daily Values are based on a 2,000 calorie diet.

Adorable Apple Pies

Ingredients

- 2 pastries for 9-inch single crust pies
- 3 C. diced Granny Smith apple
- 2 tbsp instant tapioca
- 1/2 C. white sugar
- lemon juice
- 1/8 tsp ground nutmeg
- 1/4 tsp ground cinnamon

Directions

- Set your oven to 400 degrees F before doing anything else.
- Cut about 4 (6-inch) rounds from the pie crusts.
- Arrange the crust rounds into 4 (5-inch) mini pie pans.
- Cut about 1/8-inch strips from the remaining crusts.
- In a bowl, mix together the remaining ingredients and keep aside for about 5 minutes.
- Stir the mixture well and divide it between the pie shells evenly.

- Arrange the pie strips over each pie and pinch the strips onto the bottom crust.
- Cook everything in the oven for about 30 minutes.

Amount per serving (4 total)

Timing Information:

Preparation	20 m
Cooking	30 m
Total Time	1 h 20 m

Nutritional Information:

Calories	614 kcal
Fat	29.9 g
Carbohydrates	83.1g
Protein	5.9 g
Cholesterol	0 mg
Sodium	469 mg

* Percent Daily Values are based on a 2,000 calorie diet.

ADDICTING APPLE SNACK

Ingredients

- 1/2 C. melted butter
- 1 C. white sugar
- 1 egg
- 1 C. all-purpose flour
- 1/2 tsp baking soda
- 1 tsp ground cinnamon
- 1 C. apples - peeled, cored and finely diced
- 1 C. chopped walnuts

Directions

- Set your oven to 350 degrees F before doing anything else and grease and flour an 8x8-inch baking dish.
- In a large bowl, mix together the butter, egg and sugar.
- Add the flour, baking soda and cinnamon and mix till well combined.

- Fold in the apples and walnuts and transfer the mixture onto the prepared baking dish evenly.
- Cook everything in the oven for about 40 minutes.

Amount per serving (9 total)

Timing Information:

Preparation	15 m
Cooking	40 m
Total Time	55 m

Nutritional Information:

Calories	328 kcal
Fat	19.4 g
Carbohydrates	36.8g
Protein	4.3 g
Cholesterol	48 mg
Sodium	151 mg

* Percent Daily Values are based on a 2,000 calorie diet.

OUTSTANDING APPLE DESSERT

Ingredients

- 2 tsp salt
- 4 C. all-purpose flour
- 1 1/3 C. shortening
- 2 egg yolks, beaten
- 1/2 C. milk

- 10 apples - peeled, cored and sliced
- 2 tbsp all-purpose flour
- 3 C. white sugar
- 1 tbsp ground cinnamon
- 1 egg white

Directions

- Set your oven to 375 degrees F before doing anything else and grease a 15x10-inch jelly roll pan.
- In a large bowl, add 4 C. of the flour and salt.
- With a pastry cutter, cut the shortening and mix till a crumbly mixture forms.
- Add the milk and egg yolks and mix till a dough forms.
- Divide the dough into 2 portions and place one part of the dough onto a lightly floured surface.

- With a rolling pin, roll the dough into a 1/8-inch thickness.
- Arrange the rolled dough portion in the bottom of the prepared pan.
- Place the apple slices over the crust evenly.
- In a bowl, mix together 2 tbsp of the flour, cinnamon and sugar and sprinkle everything over the apple slices evenly.
- Now, roll the remaining dough portions and place everything over the apple slices.
- With your hands, pinch the ends to seal and trim the excess crust.
- Coat with the egg white evenly and cook everything in the oven for about 40-45 minutes.
- Remove everything from the oven and keep aside to cool completely.
- With a sharp knife cut into desired squares and serve.

Amount per serving (20 total)

Timing Information:

Preparation	30 m
Cooking	45 m
Total Time	1 h 15 m

Nutritional Information:

Calories	377 kcal
Fat	14.6 g
Carbohydrates	59.8g
Protein	3.5 g
Cholesterol	21 mg
Sodium	240 mg

* Percent Daily Values are based on a 2,000 calorie diet.

BLONDE APPLE BROWNIES

Ingredients

- 1/2 C. butter, melted
- 1 C. white sugar
- 1 egg
- 3 medium apples - peeled, cored and thinly sliced
- 1/2 C. chopped walnuts
- 1 C. all-purpose flour
- 1/4 tsp salt
- 1/2 tsp baking powder
- 1/2 tsp baking soda
- 1 tsp ground cinnamon

Directions

- Set your oven to 350 degrees F before doing anything else and grease and flour a 9x9-inch baking dish.
- In a bowl, add the melted butter, egg and sugar and beat till fluffy.

- In another bowl, sift together the flour, baking soda, baking powder, cinnamon and salt.
- Add the egg mixture into the flour mixture and mix till well combined.
- Fold in the apples and walnuts and transfer the mixture onto the prepared baking dish evenly.
- Cook everything in the oven for about 35 minutes.

Amount per serving (12 total)

Timing Information:

Preparation	25 m
Cooking	35 m
Total Time	1 h

Nutritional Information:

Calories	227 kcal
Fat	11.5 g
Carbohydrates	30.3g
Protein	2.5 g
Cholesterol	36 mg
Sodium	177 mg

* Percent Daily Values are based on a 2,000 calorie diet.

APPLE CAKE IN ROMANIAN STYLE

Ingredients

- 5 apples, peeled, cored and cut into 1-inch wedges
- 3 eggs
- 1 1/2 C. white sugar
- 3/4 C. vegetable oil
- 1 tsp baking soda
- 1 tsp ground cinnamon
- 1 tbsp vanilla extract
- 2 C. all-purpose flour
- 3/4 C. chopped walnuts

Directions

- Set your oven to 350 degrees F before doing anything else and grease and flour a 13x9-inch baking dish.
- In a large bowl, add the sugar and eggs and beat till well combined.
- Add the flour, baking soda, cinnamon, oil and vanilla and mix till well combined.

- Fold in the apples and walnuts and transfer the mixture onto the prepared baking dish evenly.
- Cook everything in the oven for about 55 minutes.

Amount per serving (12 total)

Timing Information:

Preparation	20 m
Cooking	55 m
Total Time	1 h 15 m

Nutritional Information:

Calories	393 kcal
Fat	20.1 g
Carbohydrates	50.2g
Protein	5 g
Cholesterol	46 mg
Sodium	124 mg

* Percent Daily Values are based on a 2,000 calorie diet.

CRUNCHY APPLE COBBLER

Ingredients

- 4 C. thinly sliced apples
- 1/2 C. white sugar
- 1/2 tsp ground cinnamon
- 1/2 C. chopped pecans
- 1 C. all-purpose flour
- 1 C. white sugar
- 1 tsp baking powder
- 1/4 tsp salt
- 1 egg, beaten
- 1/2 C. evaporated milk
- 1/3 C. butter, melted
- 1/4 C. chopped pecans

Directions

- Set your oven to 325 degrees F before doing anything else and grease a large baking dish.
- In the bottom of the prepared baking dish, place the apple slices in a single layer.
- In a bowl, mix together the 1/2 C. of the pecans, 1/2 C. of the sugar and cinnamon and spread everything over the apple slices.
- In a second bowl, mix together the flour, baking powder, 1 C. of the sugar and salt.

- In a third bowl, add the evaporated milk, egg and melted butter and beat till well combined.
- Add the egg mixture into the flour mixture and mix till well combined.
- Place the flour mixture over the apples and sprinkle everything with the remaining pecans evenly.
- Cook everything in the oven for about 55 minutes.

Amount per serving (8 total)

Timing Information:

Preparation	30 m
Cooking	55 m
Total Time	1 h 25 m

Nutritional Information:

Calories	404 kcal
Fat	17.1 g
Carbohydrates	61.4g
Protein	4.7 g
Cholesterol	48 mg
Sodium	214 mg

* Percent Daily Values are based on a 2,000 calorie diet.

NUTRITIOUS APPLE COBBLER

Ingredients

- 3 large Granny Smith apples, peeled and sliced
- 3/4 C. white sugar
- 2 tbsp ground cinnamon
- 1 tsp ground nutmeg
- 2 tbsp lemon juice
- 1/4 C. butter, softened
- 3/4 C. white sugar
- 1 egg
- 2 C. all-purpose flour
- 2 tsp baking powder
- 1/4 tsp salt
- 1/2 C. milk
- 2 C. fresh blueberries
- 2/3 C. white sugar
- 1/2 C. all-purpose flour
- 1 tsp ground cinnamon
- 1/3 C. cold butter

Directions

- Set your oven to 375 degrees F before doing anything else and lightly, grease a 13x9-inch baking dish.
- In a bowl, add the apples, lemon juice, 3/4 C. of the sugar, 2 tbsp of the cinnamon and nutmeg and toss to coat well.
- Refrigerate, covered till ready for serving.

- In a bowl, add the softened butter and 3/4 C. of the sugar and beat till smooth and creamy.
- Add the eggs and beat till well combined.
- In another bowl, mix together 2 C. of the flour, baking powder and salt.
- Add the egg mixture into the flour mixture and mix till well combined.
- Fold in the blueberries.
- In the bottom of the prepared baking dish, place the apple slices in a single layer and top with the blueberry mixture evenly.
- In a third bowl, mix together the remaining flour, sugar and cinnamon.
- With a pastry cutter, cut the butter and mix till a crumbly mixture forms.
- Spread the mixture over the blueberry mixture evenly and cook everything in the oven for about 40-45 minutes.

Amount per serving (15 total)

Timing Information:

Preparation	30 m
Cooking	40 m
Total Time	1 h 10 m

Nutritional Information:

Calories	294 kcal
Fat	8 g
Carbohydrates	54.6g
Protein	3.2 g
Cholesterol	32 mg
Sodium	164 mg

* Percent Daily Values are based on a 2,000 calorie diet.

APPLE CAKE IN OLD-ENGLISH STYLE

Ingredients

- 1 tbsp butter, melted
- 1 (1 lb.) loaf white bread, crusts trimmed
- 8 apples - peeled, cored and chopped
- 1/3 C. white sugar
- 1/2 tbsp ground cinnamon
- 1 tbsp lemon juice
- 2 tbsp butter, cubed
- nonstick cooking spray

Directions

- Set your oven to 400 degrees F before doing anything else and grease a 9x5-inch loaf pan with melted butter.
- Arrange the required bread slices in the bottom and the sides of the prepared loaf pan evenly.
- In a bowl, mix together the remaining ingredients and place over the bread slices.

- Cover the apple mixture with the remaining bread slices and drizzle with the cooking spray.
- Cover with a sheet of foil and cook everything in the oven for about 35-40 minutes.
- Remove everything from the oven and keep aside for about 15 minutes to cool.

Amount per serving (8 total)

Timing Information:

Preparation	15 m
Cooking	45 m
Total Time	1 h

Nutritional Information:

Calories	295 kcal
Fat	6.4 g
Carbohydrates	56.6g
Protein	4.8 g
Cholesterol	11 mg
Sodium	419 mg

* Percent Daily Values are based on a 2,000 calorie diet.

SPECTACULAR APPLE & CHEESE CASSEROLE

Ingredients

- 1 C. white sugar
- 1/2 C. butter, softened
- 3/4 C. all-purpose flour
- 1/2 lb. processed cheese food, cut into small chunks
- 1 (16 oz.) can sliced apples, undrained

Directions

- Set your oven to 350 degrees F before doing anything else.
- In a bowl, add the butter and sugar and beat till smooth and creamy.
- Add the flour and beat till well combined.
- Fold in the cheese.
- In the bottom of a 13x9-inch baking dish, arrange the apple slices.
- Place the cheese mixture over the apple slices evenly.
- Cook everything in the oven for about 35-40 minutes.

Amount per serving (12 total)

Timing Information:

Preparation	15 m
Cooking	35 m
Total Time	50 m

Nutritional Information:

Calories	249 kcal
Fat	12.6 g
Carbohydrates	30.5g
Protein	4.7 g
Cholesterol	32 mg
Sodium	239 mg

* Percent Daily Values are based on a 2,000 calorie diet.

SUMMERTIME APPLE SALAD

Ingredients

- 2 C. shredded napa cabbage
- 1 (1 lb.) jicama, peeled and shredded
- 2 C. shredded daikon radish
- 2 Granny Smith apples - peeled, cored and shredded
- 2 large carrots, shredded
- 1 firm pear, shredded
- 1/4 C. finely chopped cilantro
- 2 tbsp olive oil
- 3 tbsp orange juice
- 1 tbsp lime juice
- sea salt and pepper to taste

Directions

- In a large bowl, add all the ingredients and toss to coat well.
- Serve immediately.

Amount per serving (8 total)

Timing Information:

Preparation	30 m
Cooking	30 m
Total Time	30 m

Nutritional Information:

Calories	98 kcal
Fat	3.6 g
Carbohydrates	16.8g
Protein	1.2 g
Cholesterol	0 mg
Sodium	64 mg

* Percent Daily Values are based on a 2,000 calorie diet.

Autumn Apple Salad

Ingredients

- 3 tbsp raisins
- 2 tart apples, peeled and shredded
- 1 C. shredded pumpkin
- 2 tsp lemon juice
- salt and pepper to taste

Directions

- In a bowl of hot water, soak the raisins and keep aside, covered for about 30 minutes.
- Drain well and transfer into a large bowl.
- Add the remaining ingredients and toss to coat well.
- Serve immediately.

Amount per serving (2 total)

Timing Information:

Preparation	10 m
Cooking	40 m
Total Time	50 m

Nutritional Information:

Calories	129 kcal
Fat	0.3 g
Carbohydrates	34.2g
Protein	1.2 g
Cholesterol	0 mg
Sodium	197 mg

* Percent Daily Values are based on a 2,000 calorie diet.

Asian Apple Slaw

Ingredients

- 6 tbsp rice wine vinegar
- 6 tbsp olive oil
- 5 tbsp creamy peanut butter
- 3 tbsp soy sauce
- 3 tbsp brown sugar
- 2 tbsp minced fresh ginger root
- 1 1/2 tbsp minced garlic
- 1/2 head red cabbage, finely shredded
- 2 Fuji apples - peeled, cored, and finely diced
- 1/4 C. finely minced white onion

Directions

- In a large bowl, mix together the apples, cabbage and onion.
- In another bowl, add the remaining ingredients and beat till well combined and smooth.
- Pour the dressing over salad and toss to coat well.
- Refrigerate to chill before serving.

Amount per serving (6 total)

Timing Information:

Preparation	25 m
Cooking	45 m
Total Time	1h 5 m

Nutritional Information:

Calories	282 kcal
Fat	20.6 g
Carbohydrates	23.1g
Protein	5.3 g
Cholesterol	0 mg
Sodium	536 mg

* Percent Daily Values are based on a 2,000 calorie diet.

Unique Flavored Apple Cookies

Ingredients

- 1/2 C. unsalted butter
- 1 egg yolk
- 1 C. chopped pecans
- 3/4 tsp vanilla extract
- 1/2 C. white sugar
- 1 C. all-purpose flour
- 1/2 C. toasted wheat germ
- 1/4 tsp salt
- 1/3 C. apple butter

Directions

- Set your oven to 350 degrees F before doing anything else.
- In a bowl, add the butter, egg whites and vanilla extract and beat till smooth and creamy.
- In a food processor, add the pecans and sugar and pulse till a fine texture forms.

- Add the flour, wheat germ and salt and pulse till well combined.
- Add the flour mixture into the butter mixture and mix till a dough forms.
- Make 1-inch balls from the dough and arrange onto the cookie sheets in a single layer about 2-inches apart.
- With your thumbs, create a dent on the top of each ball.
- Cook everything in the oven for about 15-20 minutes.
- Remove everything from the oven and with a spoon, open the vents.
- Keep on wire racks to cool completely.
- Fill each vent with the apple butter and serve.

Amount per serving (12 total)

Timing Information:

Preparation	15m
Cooking	20m
Total Time	35m

Nutritional Information:

Calories	237 kcal
Fat	15.2 g
Carbohydrates	23.3g
Protein	3.6 g
Cholesterol	37 mg
Sodium	52 mg

* Percent Daily Values are based on a 2,000 calorie diet.

CHEWY APPLE COOKIES

Ingredients

- 1C. sifted all-purpose flour
- 1 tsp baking powder
- 1/2 tsp salt
- 1 tsp ground cinnamon
- 1/2 tsp ground nutmeg
- 1/2 C. shortening
- 3/4 C. white sugar
- 2 eggs
- 1 C. chopped walnuts
- 1 C. apples - peeled, cored and finely diced
- 1 C. rolled oats

Directions

- Set your oven to 350 degrees F before doing anything else.
- In a large bowl, mix together the flour, baking powder, cinnamon, nutmeg and salt.
- In another bowl, add the shortening and white sugar and beat till smooth and creamy.
- Add the eggs and beat till well combined.
- Add the egg mixture into the flour mixture and mix till well combined.
- Fold in the oats, apples and walnuts.

- With a spoon, place the mixture onto the cookie sheets in a single layer about 2-inches apart.
- Cook everything in the oven for about 12-15 minutes.
- Remove everything from the oven and keep it all on wire racks to cool completely.

Amount per serving (36 total)

Timing Information:

Preparation	20m
Cooking	15m
Total Time	40m

Nutritional Information:

Calories	90 kcal
Fat	5.4 g
Carbohydrates	9.4g
Protein	1.5 g
Cholesterol	10 mg
Sodium	50 mg

* Percent Daily Values are based on a 2,000 calorie diet.

HOME-STYLE APPLE DESSERT

Ingredients

- 1 C. all-purpose flour
- 3/4 C. packed brown sugar
- 1/2 C. rolled oats
- 1/4 C. graham cracker crumbs
- 1 tsp ground cinnamon
- 1/2 C. melted butter
- 3 1/2 C. peeled and sliced apples
- 1 1/2 C. blueberries
- 1 tbsp lemon juice
- 1/4 C. white sugar
- 2 tbsp cornstarch
- 1 C. cold water
- 1 tsp vanilla extract

Directions

- Grease a large microwave safe casserole dish.
- In a large bowl, mix together the flour, oats, brown sugar, crackers and cinnamon.
- Add the butter and mix till well combined.
- Place half of the flour mixture in the bottom of the prepared casserole dish evenly.

- Place the apples and blueberries over the flour mixture evenly and drizzle with the lemon juice.
- In a microwave safe bowl, mix together cornstarch, white sugar, vanilla extract and water.
- Microwave on high for about 2-4 minutes, stirring every 45 seconds.
- Pour the cornstarch mixture over the fruit layer evenly and top with the remaining flour mixture.
- Cook everything in the oven for about 25 minutes.
- Remove everything from the oven and keep aside to cool slightly.

Amount per serving (8 total)

Timing Information:

Preparation	20 m
Cooking	10 m
Total Time	30 m

Nutritional Information:

Calories	346 kcal
Fat	12.4 g
Carbohydrates	57.6g
Protein	3 g
Cholesterol	31 mg
Sodium	106 mg

* Percent Daily Values are based on a 2,000 calorie diet.

Festive Apple Treat

Ingredients

- 5 large Granny Smith apples
- wooden craft sticks
- 1 (14 oz.) package individually wrapped caramels, unwrapped
- 2 tbsp water
- 7 oz. chocolate candy bar, broken into pieces
- 2 tbsp shortening, divided
- 1 C. colored candy coating melts

Directions

- In a large pan of boiling water, dip the apples for a while.
- With a slotted spoon remove everything from the water and pat them dry.
- Line a cookie sheet with greased foil.
- In the core of each apple, insert a wooden stick at the stem end.
- Arrange the apples onto the prepared cookie sheet.

- In a microwave safe bowl, add the caramel and water and microwave on high for about 2 minutes.
- Stir well and microwave on high till melted completely, stirring every 1 minute.
- Dip the apples in the caramel mixture evenly.
- In a microwave safe bowl, add the chocolate candy bar and 1 tbsp of the shortening and microwave on high till melted completely.
- Dip the apples in the chocolate mixture evenly.
- In a microwave safe bowl, add the candy coating and the remaining shortening and microwave on high till melted completely, stirring every 30 seconds.
- Dip a fork in the coating mixture and make designs on apples and refrigerate till set.

Amount per serving (5 total)

Timing Information:

Preparation	5 m
Cooking	45 m
Total Time	50 m

Nutritional Information:

Calories	831 kcal
Fat	34.8 g
Carbohydrates	131.6g
Protein	8.1 g
Cholesterol	22 mg
Sodium	249 mg

* Percent Daily Values are based on a 2,000 calorie diet.

CRUNCHY APPLES

Ingredients

- 6 Granny Smith apples
- 6 wooden sticks
- 1 (14 oz.) package individually wrapped caramels, unwrapped
- 2 tbsp water
- 1/2 tsp vanilla extract
- 3 C. chopped peanut butter filled sandwich cookies
- 4 oz. milk chocolate, chopped
- 4 oz. white chocolate, chopped

Directions

- Line a cookie sheet with greased foil.
- In the core of each apple, insert a wooden stick at the stem end.
- Arrange the apples onto the prepared cookie sheet.
- In a pan, mix together the water and caramel on low heat.
- Cook, stirring occasionally till caramel are melted completely.
- Stir in the vanilla extract and remove from the heat.

- Dip the apples in the caramel mixture evenly.
- In a shallow dish, place the cookies.
- Roll the apples into cookies evenly and arrange onto the cookie sheet.
- In 2 microwave safe bowl, add both the chocolate chips separately and microwave on high till melted completely, stirring every 30 seconds.
- Pour the melted milk chocolate over apples, followed by the white chocolate chips and refrigerate till set.

Amount per serving (6 total)

Timing Information:

Preparation	25 m
Cooking	10 m
Total Time	35 m

Nutritional Information:

Calories	704 kcal
Fat	25.3 g
Carbohydrates	116g
Protein	9.5 g
Cholesterol	13 mg
Sodium	341 mg

* Percent Daily Values are based on a 2,000 calorie diet.

SENSATIONAL APPLES

Ingredients

- 6 Granny Smith apples
- 6 wooden sticks
- 1 (14 oz.) package individually wrapped caramels, unwrapped
- 2 tbsp water
- 1/2 tsp vanilla extract
- 1 1/2 tbsp coarse sea salt
- 1 C. semisweet chocolate chips

Directions

- Line a cookie sheet with greased foil.
- In the core of each apple, insert a wooden stick at the stem end.
- Arrange the apples onto the prepared cookie sheet.
- In a pan, mix together the water and caramel on low heat.
- Cook, stirring occasionally till the caramel is melted completely.
- Stir in the vanilla extract and remove from the heat.

- Dip the apples in the caramel mixture evenly and arrange onto the cookie sheet.
- Sprinkle with the salt and refrigerate to chill.
- In a microwave safe bowl, add the chocolate chips and microwave on high till melted completely, stirring every 30 seconds.
- Pour the melted chocolate over the apples and refrigerate till everything is set.

Amount per serving (6 total)

Timing Information:

Preparation	15m
Cooking	10m
Total Time	30m

Nutritional Information:

Calories	445 kcal
Fat	13.7 g
Carbohydrates	85.1g
Protein	4.6 g
Cholesterol	5 mg
Sodium	1485 mg

* Percent Daily Values are based on a 2,000 calorie diet.

OLD-TIMED BAKED APPLES

Ingredients

- 4 tart green apples
- 1/2 C. brown sugar
- 4 tbsp butter
- 2 tsp ground cinnamon

Directions

- Set your oven to 350 degrees F before doing anything else.
- Scoop out the core of each apple from the top, leaving a well.
- Fill each apple well with 2 tbsp of the brown sugar and 1 tbsp of the butter.
- In a shallow baking dish, arrange the apples and sprinkle them with the cinnamon evenly.
- Cook everything in the oven for about 15 minutes.

Amount per serving (4 total)

Timing Information:

Preparation	15 m
Cooking	15 m
Total Time	30 m

Nutritional Information:

Calories	270 kcal
Fat	11.5 g
Carbohydrates	45g
Protein	0.6 g
Cholesterol	31 mg
Sodium	91 mg

* Percent Daily Values are based on a 2,000 calorie diet.

APPLE TREAT FOR CHOCOLATE LOVERS

Ingredients

- 10 small Granny Smith apples
- 1/2 C. chopped roasted peanuts
- 1/2 C. candy-coated milk chocolate candies
- 2 lb. semisweet chocolate, chopped

Directions

- In the core of each apple, insert a lollipop stick at the stem end.
- In 2 shallow dishes, place the peanuts and candies separately.
- In a pan of simmering water, arrange a heatproof glass bowl.
- Add the chocolate chips and stir continuously till everything melts completely.
- Coat the apples with the melted chocolate evenly and roll them in the peanuts followed by the candies.
- Place the apples on a wax paper lined baking sheet and keep aside for about 20 minutes.

Amount per serving (10 total)

Timing Information:

Preparation	30 m
Cooking	1 h
Total Time	1 h 30 m

Nutritional Information:

Calories	589 kcal
Fat	34.6 g
Carbohydrates	73.3g
Protein	8.9 g
Cholesterol	1 mg
Sodium	67 mg

* Percent Daily Values are based on a 2,000 calorie diet.

Deep South Fried Maple Apples

Ingredients

- 5 apples - peeled, cored and sliced
- 1/4 C. vegetable oil
- 1/4 C. maple flavored syrup
- 1 pinch salt

Directions

- In a cast iron pan, heat the oil on medium heat and cook the apple slices till soft on both sides.
- Sprinkle everything with salt and drizzle the maple syrup over everything.

Amount per serving (4 total)

Timing Information:

Preparation	10m
Cooking	10m
Total Time	20m

Nutritional Information:

Calories	263 kcal
Fat	14.1 g
Carbohydrates	37.5g
Protein	0.4 g
Cholesterol	0 mg
Sodium	111 mg

* Percent Daily Values are based on a 2,000 calorie diet.

Apple Soup For Cold Fall Nights

Ingredients

- 1 tbsp reduced-fat margarine
- 3 tart apples - peeled, cored, and chopped
- 3 pears - peeled, cored, and chopped
- 5 C. vegetable broth
- 1/2 tsp rubbed sage
- 1/4 tsp ground black pepper
- 1 bay leaf
- 1 1/2 tsp pureed fresh ginger
- 1 tbsp chopped fresh parsley

Directions

- In a large pan, melt the margarine on medium heat and cook the apples and peas for about 5 minutes.
- Add the broth, sage, bay leaf and pepper and bring everything to a boil.
- Reduce the heat to low and simmer, covered for about 20 minutes.

- Remove everything from the heat and keep aside for about 5 minutes to cool.
- In a blender, add the soup mixture in batches and pulse till smooth.
- Return the soup in the pan on medium heat and cook till heated completely.
- Serve with a topping of parsley.

Amount per serving (7 total)

Timing Information:

Preparation	20 m
Cooking	35 m
Total Time	1 h

Nutritional Information:

Calories	102 kcal
Fat	1.3 g
Carbohydrates	22.9g
Protein	1.2 g
Cholesterol	0 mg
Sodium	349 mg

* Percent Daily Values are based on a 2,000 calorie diet.

IRRESISTIBLY CRISPY APPLE PANCAKES

Ingredients

- 3 russet potatoes, peeled and shredded
- 1 Granny Smith apple - peeled, cored, and shredded
- 2 eggs
- 2 tbsp all-purpose flour
- 3 green onions, diced
- salt to taste
- vegetable oil for frying, or as needed
- 1/2 tbsp sour cream

Directions

- Squeeze the apple and potato to drain the excess moisture.
- In a bowl, mix together the apple, potatoes, green onion, flour and eggs.
- In a large heavy skillet, heat the oil on medium-high heat.
- Divide the mixture into palm sized patties and cook everything for about 2-4 minutes per side. (Cook the dish in batches).

- Transfer the pancakes onto a paper towel lined plate and sprinkle with the salt.
- Serve with a topping of the sour cream.

Amount per serving (5 total)

Timing Information:

Preparation	20 m
Cooking	20 m
Total Time	40 m

Nutritional Information:

Calories	178 kcal
Fat	4.7 g
Carbohydrates	29.4g
Protein	5.7 g
Cholesterol	75 mg
Sodium	69 mg

* Percent Daily Values are based on a 2,000 calorie diet.

IRISH APPLE MASH

Ingredients

- 2 C. water, divided
- 1 tsp brown sugar
- 1 small lemon, halved and juiced, halves reserved
- 1 large apple (such as Honey Crisp), peeled and chopped
- 4 large baking potatoes, peeled and chopped
- 6 C. water
- 3 tbsp butter
- 3 tbsp heavy whipping cream
- 1 tsp salt
- 1 tbsp ground black pepper

Directions

- In a pan, mix together the apple, reserved lemon halves, brown sugar, lemon juice and 2 C. of the water on medium-high heat.
- Boil for about 10-12 minutes and drain well, then transfer into a large bowl.

- Discard the lemon halves and keep the apple slices warm by covering them with foil.
- In a large pan, add the potatoes and 6 C. of the water on medium-high heat.
- Cook everything for 15-20 minutes and drain well.
- Add the potatoes in the bowl with the apple and with a hand blender mash them completely.

Amount per serving (6 total)

Timing Information:

Preparation	15 m
Cooking	25 m
Total Time	40 m

Nutritional Information:

Calories	293 kcal
Fat	8.9 g
Carbohydrates	51g
Protein	5.6 g
Cholesterol	25 mg
Sodium	457 mg

* Percent Daily Values are based on a 2,000 calorie diet.

THANKSGIVING FAVORITE APPLE DESSERT

Ingredients

- 2 large sweet potatoes, peeled and diced
- 2 large Honeycrisp apples, diced
- 2 tsp ground cinnamon
- 1/2 tsp ground nutmeg
- 2/3 C. water
- 2 tbsp butter, diced

Directions

- Set your oven to 425 degrees F before doing anything else.
- In the bottom of a microwave safe loaf pan, arrange the sweet potatoes and apples and sprinkle them with nutmeg and cinnamon.
- Add enough water to cover about 1/2-inch of the bottom and cook everything in the microwave for about 8 minutes.
- Drain well.

- Place the butter over the apple mixture in the shape of dots and cook everything in the oven for about 10 minutes.

Amount per serving (8 total)

Timing Information:

Preparation	10 m
Cooking	20 m
Total Time	30 m

Nutritional Information:

Calories	153 kcal
Fat	3.1 g
Carbohydrates	30.7g
Protein	2 g
Cholesterol	8 mg
Sodium	84 mg

* Percent Daily Values are based on a 2,000 calorie diet.

REFRESHING APPLE JUICE

Ingredients

- 4 carrots, trimmed
- 2 apples, quartered
- 2 stalks celery
- 1 (1/2 inch) piece fresh ginger

Directions

- In a juicer, add all the ingredients except the ginger and process according to manufacturer's directions.
- Add the ginger and process again.

Amount per serving (1 total)

Timing Information:

Preparation	10 m
Cooking	10 m
Total Time	10 m

Nutritional Information:

Calories	277 kcal
Fat	1.3 g
Carbohydrates	68.6g
Protein	4 g
Cholesterol	0 mg
Sodium	266 mg

* Percent Daily Values are based on a 2,000 calorie diet.

Traditional Autumn Sweet Treat

Ingredients

- 4 1/2 C. peeled, cored and sliced apples
- 2 tsp lemon juice
- 2 tbsp water
- 3/4 C. brown sugar
- 3/4 C. all-purpose flour
- 3/4 C. rolled oats
- 4 tbsp butter

Directions

- Set your oven to 350 degrees F before doing anything else and lightly, grease a casserole dish.
- Place the apple slices in the bottom of the prepared casserole dish evenly.
- In a bowl, mix together the water and lemon juice and drizzle over the apple slices evenly.

- In another bowl, add the remaining ingredients and mix till a coarse crumb forms.
- Spread the crumb mixture over the apple slices evenly and cook everything in the oven for about 25 minutes.

Amount per serving (8 total)

Timing Information:

Preparation	35 m
Cooking	25 m
Total Time	1 h

Nutritional Information:

Calories	298 kcal
Fat	6.5 g
Carbohydrates	60.7g
Protein	2.5 g
Cholesterol	15 mg
Sodium	49 mg

* Percent Daily Values are based on a 2,000 calorie diet.

Awesome Apple Glaze for Ham

Ingredients

- 1 C. apple butter
- 1/2 C. orange juice
- 1 tbsp dried onion flakes
- 1 tbsp Worcestershire sauce

Directions

- In a pan, add all the ingredients and simmer till thickened.

Amount per serving (12 total)

Timing Information:

Preparation	5 m
Cooking	5 m
Total Time	10 m

Nutritional Information:

Calories	47 kcal
Fat	0.1 g
Carbohydrates	11.6g
Protein	0.2 g
Cholesterol	0 mg
Sodium	18 mg

* Percent Daily Values are based on a 2,000 calorie diet.

FAMILY FAVORITE APPLE SPREAD

Ingredients

- 1 (8 oz.) package light cream cheese, softened
- 1/2 C. apple butter
- 1/2 tsp vanilla extract
- 1 pinch ground cinnamon

Directions

- In a food processor, add the apple butter, cream cheese, vanilla and cinnamon and pulse till smooth.
- Transfer the mixture into a bowl and refrigerate, covered for about 30 minutes.

Amount per serving (12 total)

Timing Information:

Preparation	5 m
Cooking	35 m
Total Time	45 m

Nutritional Information:

Calories	65 kcal
Fat	3.4 g
Carbohydrates	6.4g
Protein	2.1 g
Cholesterol	11 mg
Sodium	58 mg

* Percent Daily Values are based on a 2,000 calorie diet.

APPLE BRINE FOR THANKSGIVING

Ingredients

- 1/4 C. dried rosemary
- 1/4 C. ground thyme
- 2 tbsp rubbed sage
- 4 bay leaves
- 1 tsp ground black pepper
- 1 gallon boiling water
- 1 lb. kosher salt
- 1 gallon cold apple juice

Directions

- In a cloth spice bag, add the herbs, bay leaves and black pepper.
- In a large pan, add the water and salt and mix till the salt is dissolved completely.
- Bring everything to a boil and add the spice bag and simmer for about 20 minutes.

- Remove everything from the heat and keep aside for about 1 hour to cool completely.
- Stir in the cold apple juice.

Amount per serving (1 total)

Timing Information:

Preparation	15 m
Cooking	30 m
Total Time	1 h 45 m

Nutritional Information:

Calories	1964 kcal
Fat	8.2 g
Carbohydrates	484.3g
Protein	15.3 g
Cholesterol	0 mg
Sodium	1849 mg

* Percent Daily Values are based on a 2,000 calorie diet.

THANKS FOR READING! NOW LET'S TRY SOME **SUSHI** AND **DUMP DINNERS**....

http://bit.ly/2443TFg

To grab this **box set** simply follow the link mentioned above, or tap the book cover.

This will take you to a page where you can simply enter your email address and a PDF version of the **box set** will be emailed to you.

I hope you are ready for some serious cooking!

http://bit.ly/2443TFg

You will also receive updates about all my new books when they are free.

Also don't forget to like and subscribe on the social networks. I love meeting my readers. Links to all my profiles are below so please click and connect :)

Facebook

Twitter

Come On...
Let's Be Friends :)

I adore my readers and love connecting with them socially. Please follow the links below so we can connect on Facebook, Twitter, and Google+.

Facebook

Twitter

I also have a blog that I regularly update for my readers so check it out below.

My Blog

Can I Ask A Favour?

If you found this book interesting, or have otherwise found any benefit in it. Then may I ask that you post a review of it on Amazon? Nothing excites me more than new reviews, especially reviews which suggest new topics for writing. I do read all reviews and I always factor feedback into my newer works.

So if you are willing to take ten minutes to write what you sincerely thought about this book then please visit our Amazon page and post your opinions.

Again thank you!

Interested in Other Easy Cookbooks?

Everything is easy! Check out my Amazon Author page for more great cookbooks:

For a complete listing of all my books please see my author page.

Printed by Amazon Italia Logistica S.r.l.
Torrazza Piemonte (TO), Italy